Getting My Life On Track

By Allen L. Elder

ISBN: 978-1-7059-0344-5

DEDICATION

This book is dedicated to Herb Hodges who helped me get
my life on track.

Table of Contents

INTRODUCTION

The most wonderful thing in the world is to know that you have a personal relationship with the Almighty God on his terms. The most frustrating thing in the world is to not have your life on track in that glorious relationship. Many believers live their entire life as a Christian never knowing what their life in Christ Jesus is all about and never becoming all they could become in this world for God. This little book is an effort to correct this problem in your life.

This book points out four basic pillars on which you can build for the rest of your life on earth. One pillar on each corner of your life provides the stability you will need for constant and continual growth from now on. Finding these pillars is the first step toward getting your life on track with God. Building upon these pillars will keep your life on track. And when you feel like your life is a little off track, you can always come back to these four pillars to get on track again. It really is that simple.

Now, let's see what we can do to get your life on track starting right now.

Allen L. Elder

1. MY PERSONAL RELATIONSHIP WITH GOD

LESSON AIM: To give a clear presentation of the gospel of Jesus Christ.

This book could have been called by several other titles. It could have been called "Four Pillars of the Christian Life", "Walking with God", "Living a Biblical Life", or a dozen other like titles. I called it "Getting Your Life On Track" because the reality for many Christians is that their life is off the rails and getting it on track is what they desperately need and hope to do.

The Bible and the Christian life are at the same time the most simple thing and the most complicated thing anything could possibly be. As a Bible teacher and communicator of God's Word, I am always looking for the most simple way to explain the most complicated ideas. The four lessons presented in this book are really what the Christian life is all about in simple terms. Any doctrine or theological concept we might name could be a part of one of these four pillars. Therefore, if we can get these pillars set in our mind and heart, we can get our life on track and we can build on these ideas for the rest of our life. To do this is the intention of this book.

These four lessons tell us, in a nut shell, what Christians ought to be concerned with: salvation, spiritual growth, personal ministry, and impacting the lives of

1

others through evangelism and disciple-making. This basic overview will help us to get and keep ourselves on the right track of being involved in the important things in life. It will also guide us toward working to involve other people in the same process. Let's begin by looking at what the Word of God says about eternal salvation.

The created world is a beautiful thing. We have all seen wondrous beauty among the heavenly hosts of outer space, in the skies around our planet, from the ocean depths, and on the landscape itself. Everywhere we look there is a masterpiece in motion of creative beauty all around us.

Perhaps the most breathtaking beauty of all is found in the plain sight of daily life. It is so obvious and prevalent that we easily miss it. I am speaking of the beauty that is seen in all the peoples of the earth; the beauty of the family of mankind.

One of the most beautiful things about the nations is seen in their diversity. From some 12,000 people groups (depending upon whose groupings you read) no two of them are exactly alike. They each have those unique traits that set them apart from all the other peoples of the world. Each group has its own roots, traditions, and world view. The sum total of all these unique traits we think of as their culture.

While there are these unique traits that distinguish all the groups from the others, there are also some universal truths that can be found at the heart of every ethnic group. These are the things that are found in every group regardless of whom they are or where we may find them. These are the things that create common ground between the diverse nations of the earth. The universal truths we will address in this lesson are some of the ones we find that are of a spiritual nature. We will think of three of them.

When we hear the word "sin" we usually think of it in terms of the things we do. We think of sin as doing something bad or wrong on the shallow end and as something evil or unspeakable on the deepest end. While most of us realize we are not perfect, it is still sometimes hard even to admit that we have a problem with sin. We think of it in the lives of others perhaps as those things done on the deep end of the scale and for ourselves, those things on the shallow end. We think of ourselves as not being all that bad especially when we are compared with someone else. As long as we can think of our sin problem in this way, we can find it easy to dismiss the situation entirely from our lives. Our conclusion is that we are not that bad of a person and the things we do are not as bad as those things done by others so we are probably in pretty good shape, spiritually speaking that is.

There is another way to consider the matter of the sin problem. Instead of thinking of it initially in terms of the things we do, we need to think of it as a condition into which we are born. The wrong things we do are done not simply because we are bad people but because we find ourselves in a bad condition. And the bad condition we are in is that we have inherited a sin problem from Adam, the very first man to walk on the earth. He was the representative of the human race when he disobeyed God in the Garden of Eden (Genesis 1-3), and the sin he committed was charged to all of us. In the sight of God, we all have sinned against him. The Bible says it like this: "Therefore, as by the offense of one judgment came upon all men to condemnation" (Romans 5:18a).

When we begin to examine this condition we are in, we find that it is a terrible condition in which to be. The sin problem that we inherited from Adam has caused each one of us to die spiritually. In fact, this is the very thing that God said would happen if Adam ate from the tree that had been forbidden. God said, "In the day that you eat thereof, you will die" (Genesis 2:17). The death he was speaking of was a spiritual death. And the spiritual death was passed on to each one of us: "for as in Adam all die" (1 Corinthians 15:22a). In the New Testament, Paul spoke of us as being "dead in trespasses and in sins" (Ephesians 2:1). So the sin problem we inherited from Adam means that sin has caused us to die spiritually.

Spiritual death means that we are separated from God. The relationship man once had with God has been broken. Man no longer walks and talks with God in an up-close, personal relationship. Because of sin, man is alienated from God and is a stranger and an enemy to him. Man cannot see things from God's point of view. He cannot understand the things of God and has no understanding of his ways. Man is found to be without God and without hope apart from him (Ephesians 2:12).

To further complicate the matter, we are unable to come back to God on our own (Ephesians 2:8-9). After all, what can one do that is dead? We are unable to do anything by way of good works that would get us out of the desperate situation we are in before God. We cannot do anything or offer anything that would change God's mind toward us concerning the sin problem we have inherited from Adam. As God sees it, we are in a hopeless situation, unable to lift as much as a little finger to even contribute to our rescue from this separation from God.

Is there a way out of this condition of sin and separation from God? Can we be restored so that we can know God, and have a right relationship with him again? Yes, there is a solution! The Bible calls this the good news. It is good news because the situation we are in is the bad news. We are estranged from God and cannot come back to him on our own. We need a solution for our sin problem that will be acceptable to God on his terms. He himself has provided the solution we need and the solution is Jesus Christ. Jesus is the Son of God who came to the earth to lay down his life as a sacrifice in order to remove our problem of sin and the resulting separation from God that sin has caused. He shed his blood for us and died in our place that he might atone for our sin and reconcile us to God. He was buried and arose from the dead, proving that he was the Son of God and therefore qualified to die such a death on our behalf. This death, burial, and resurrection is the gospel, or good news, of the Lord Jesus Christ. This is the solution God has provided to bring us back into a relationship with him.

The death of Jesus is acceptable to God for our sin problem. John wrote that his death satisfied God's just and righteous demands concerning our sin (1 John 2:2a). We are unable to satisfy God for our sin, but Jesus was able, and he did all that was necessary to restore us to a right relationship with God. In the same way that Adam's sin was charged to each one of us, Jesus died for us so that his righteousness could be charged to those who believe on him and receive him in their heart. We have no righteousness of our own. The righteousness of Christ is the grounds of our new standing before God, even as much as if we had never even sinned at all.

Concerning the death of Jesus Christ and his righteousness that he transfers to us which covers, or blots out our sin before God, there is no other solution that God will accept. The name of Jesus is the only name in which we can come to God and receive his complete forgiveness and restoration (Acts 4:12). Jesus himself said, "I am the way, the truth, and the life: no man comes to the Father, but by me" (John 14:6). There is a single solution for our sin problem, and the solution is Jesus Christ. Only this solution is acceptable to God.

A story is told in the Old Testament of a great man who had been stricken with leprosy (2 Kings 5). A prophet of God told him that he could be made clean if he would dip himself seven times in the Jordan River. He was a proud man and did not want to follow the way in which God had prescribed his cleansing. He wanted to be made whole on his own terms. He went away from the prophet still covered with leprosy. His servants came to him and convinced him to swallow his pride and do as the man of God had said. He did, and he was cleansed of the disease of leprosy.

We can be cleansed of our sin problem in the same way that Naaman was cleansed of leprosy; by coming to God in the way that he has prescribed and in the way that is acceptable unto him. This way is through Jesus Christ. We can have our problem with sin dealt with once and for all, and have a right relationship with God through the work that Jesus has done on our behalf.

How can we have this wonderful experience? We can have a new life in Christ by believing on Jesus and receiving him in our heart, and by confessing with our mouth that he is the Messiah and that we are his follower (Romans 10:9-10). We can be proud, like Naaman, and try other ways to be cleansed of our sin, none of which will be acceptable to God. Or, we can come God's prescribed way, by grace through faith in the Lord Jesus Christ and have our relationship with God restored (Ephesians 2:8-9). It only makes sense to come to God in the way that he accepts so that we might be made new in his sight. "If any man is in Christ, he is a new creature: old things are passed away and all things become new" (2 Corinthians 5:17).

At The LIFE Network, we care about you. We want you to have a right relationship with God. This is the reason we have shared this good news with you. After reading and hearing this lesson, if something within you seems to be in agreement with what you have heard, I want to invite you to believe on Jesus Christ in your heart, confess him with your mouth, and receive a new life in him. I invite you to pray from your heart the following prayer to God, confessing your trust in Jesus for his salvation. Please pray these words to God.

"Dear God. I admit my separation from you because of my sin against you. I acknowledge that you sent Jesus to

bring me back to you. I believe in my heart that Jesus is the Son of God. I believe that he died for me and that he arose from the dead. I confess Jesus as Lord and Savior of my life. I repent of my sins. I receive your gift of salvation through Jesus Christ. Thank you for making me right with you. Amen."

If you prayed this prayer sincerely to God from your heart, you are now a child of God and are a part of his family. God is now your Father. We are your brothers and sisters in Christ. God wants you to grow in your relationship with him. He is working to get this same message to other people throughout the world and he has a job for you to do for him in this work. We want to help you discover what it is that he wants you to do and help you learn how to do it. Remember, as you begin to learn and grow in Christ, we are here for you to answer any of your questions and to help you along the way. Congratulations on your new relationship with God. We believe he has great things in store for you.

MY PERSONAL RELATIONSHIP WITH GOD

Spiritual truths common to all peoples:

I EVERY PERSON HAS INHERITED A SIN PROBLEM FROM ADAM
   Sin can be thought of as:
   A. The things we do
      1. Not so bad things
      2. Very bad things
   B. A condition into which we are born
      1. Spiritually dead
      2. Separated from God

7

3. Unable to come to God on our own

II WE NEED A SOLUTION FOR OUR SIN PROBLEM THAT GOD WILL ACCEPT
A. The solution is Jesus Christ
1. His death and burial
2. His resurrection
B. God accepts the death of Christ in exchange for our sin
1. Christ is the propitiation for our sin
2. God accepts no other offering

III THROUGH JESUS WE CAN HAVE A RIGHT RELATIONSHIP WITH GOD
A. Come to God on God's terms
B. Believe on Christ and be saved

SCRIPTURES TO BROADEN YOUR UNDERSTANDING
1. Sin
   Romans 3:23
   Romans 6:23
   Ephesians 3:1-3

2. All sinned in Adam
   1 Corinthians 15:22

3. Salvation
   Ephesians 2:8-9
   Romans 10:9-10
   John 1:12
   John 5:24

4. The created world
   Genesis 1-2
   Romans 1:20

GETTING MY LIFE ON TRACK

Hebrews 11:1-3

LINES OF THEOLOGICAL CONNECTION
1. SIN
   Sin
   Inherited sin
   Man's depravity

2. SOTERIOLOGY
   Atonement
   Imputed righteousness
   Redemption
   Propitiation
   Salvation by grace

LESSON GLOSSARY
1. Inherit
   To receive from one's ancestors.

2. Condemnation
   The state of being declared guilty of wrong.

3. Atone
   To make amends; to set right.

4. Reconcile
   To cause to be friendly or harmonious again.

LESSON QUESTIONS

1. What are some beautiful sights you have seen in the created world?

2. Name some things that you enjoy about people.

3. Do you know your own ethnic background?

4. List some of the ethnic groups in your community.

5. Sin is devastating, not simply because of the things we do, but because of the condition into which we are born. List three results of our sinful condition.

6. What is the only solution God will accept for our sin problem?

7. How does God's solution for our sin problem come to us?

8. Jesus died on the cross for our sins and he arose from the dead. The Bible calls this the gospel, or good news.

GETTING MY LIFE ON TRACK

List two ways that God moves us to respond to the gospel.

9. Have you believed on Jesus for salvation?

10. Would you like to speak with someone about your decision to trust Christ?

Allen L. Elder

2. MY SPIRITUAL GROWTH

LESSON AIM: Show that once we are saved, we need to grow spiritually.

When we are brought into a brand new relationship with God, we are as a new baby when it is born into the world (1 Peter 2:2). It is alive and well but completely dependent upon another human being to care for it until it matures enough to begin to take care of itself.

We have a similar situation in our lives when we begin to have children. When we bring them home from the hospital, we have to do everything for them. We have to feed them, bathe them, clothe them, teach them to walk and talk, and everything else. Eventually, they become capable of doing these things for themselves. The goal is that one day they will be able to do these things for their own children. This is how it is with new Christians. They have to grow in order to become more than they are when they are born again into God's family.

There are a number of ways that Christians refer to this process of spiritual growth. We call it growing in Christ, spiritual growth, spiritual development, maturing in Christ, and discipleship, among other things. Any one of these phrases or words refers to the same process. I personally like the term, discipleship. Before believers in God were called Christians, they were called disciples. A disciple is a learner and a follower. This definition encompasses our maturing process as well as the work we are to do for God as his followers in the world.

If a child is going to grow, he is going to have to eat. He must have a regular intake of nourishing food that will cause his physical development to take place as it should. Christians, or disciples, also need nourishing food in order to grow spiritually. The food that has been provided for our spiritual development is the Bible, God's holy word. Let's see how the Bible can help us in the process of spiritual growth and development that we might become more than we are now for the glory of God.

The Bible is not an ordinary book. In fact, it is the most unusual book in the history of the world. The thing that makes it so unusual is that it was given to us by God himself. The Bible claims for itself that it is inspired by God (2Timothy 3:16). That is, the words we are given are from the mind and mouth of God, written for us by human authors (2Peter 1:21).

The Bible was written over a period of about 1,500 years by about 40 different men. It does not tell us everything about God. It says that the world itself could not contain the books that should be written about Jesus (John 21:25). It does tell us however, enough to know that God created us, loves us, cares for us, and has done everything necessary to make us at one with him again. It tells us how to know him in an intimate way. And, it tells us enough that pertains to life and to godliness that will make it possible for us to live lives that will be pleasing to God. The information the Bible contains on these and other subjects is the food we need in order to grow spiritually.

Since the Bible is of a spiritual nature, it requires that we interact with it on a spiritual level. Spiritual things must be spiritually discerned (1Corinthians 2:14). As we interact with the word of God, we are actually interacting with God himself. The same Holy Spirit who inspired the Bible can give us the illumination we need to receive it, understand it, and apply it in our lives (Ephesians 1:17-19). Therefore when we come to read the Bible, we must come humbly and dependent upon God to help us as we read. If we come to God and the Scriptures in a proud and haughty way, or in a rebellious way, he will withhold his illumination and see that we do not get what we need from the Bible. The attitude of our heart toward God and his word conditions his response toward us in the matter of understanding the Bible. As we come to the word, we need to ask God to correct any wrong attitude within our heart and let us receive his wisdom as we read his word (1Peter 5:5-7).

The Bible was given to us that we might grow from the reading, study, and living of it. For the baby Christian, the Bible is like milk to a little baby. It has in it everything that baby Christian needs for his growth and development as an infant, to a toddler, to a child. For the maturing Christian, the same Bible is like meat that will help him develop into a strong adult for the Lord's use (Hebrews 5:13-14). In this way, the Bible can help us become much more than we are now as we learn and follow that which God reveals to us in the Bible.

There are many things that help us along the way in our spiritual growth. Among those things are Christian friends and mentors, the church, a pastor, a small group, books and other tools for the study of the Bible. The one thing that will help us the most to grow spiritually is the Bible itself. As we begin to get into the Bible, we find that in the process, the Bible, or God's word, is getting into us. By getting into us, we begin to see life and to approach life from God's point of view which is presented to us in the Bible. Before long, we are applying the Word of God to our life in the decisions that we are making and are seeking to live life after the patterns God is revealing to us from the Bible.

2 Timothy 3:16-17 names four ways the Bible helps us in our spiritual growth. It says the Scriptures are

profitable to us for doctrine, reproof, correction and instruction. Through these ministries of the Word, we mature and become equipped to do the work God has for us to do.

When we read the Word, we should try to determine these four works in the Scriptures with which we are reading. Doctrine is the body of truth which lies at the foundation of our belief. What we believe conditions how we behave. Through doctrine, God reveals his ways to us, showing us his standards which should govern our lives. Reproof is the work of the Scriptures which addresses the wrong belief or wrong behavior in which we are engaged. When the Scripture reproves us, it is telling us that either we believe something that is wrong, or we are going against a correct doctrine, or teaching, that we believe. Correction is when the Bible tells us how to fix something that is wrong. And, instruction from the Word is that which helps us stay on course. In brief, the Bible tells us what is right; what is wrong; how to make it right; and how to keep it right. As God does this work within us through the Scriptures, we can experience spiritual growth.

The only way the Bible is going to be able to help us is by our using it on a regular basis. The first thing we have to do is to read it (Colossians 4:16). Of course, the Bible can be an intimidating book, hard to read and understand. But the more we read it and get to know it, the more enjoyable it becomes to read it and to learn more from it. We have to discipline ourselves to spend some time taking in God's Word. There is no substitute for it whatsoever.

Next, as we read the Bible, we have to believe it (Hebrews 11:6). We have to take God at his word. We cannot believe it and reject it at the same time. There will be parts of it that we will have to wrestle with, but this is alright. The wrestling will help us consider all the angles and know why we believe the Word. This in turn will equip us to explain things to other people who are wrestling with the same issues.

We have to study the Bible (2Timothy 2:15). The Bible is a very simple book on the one hand and very complex on the other hand. It has a unique structure that is revealing in itself as to how God works in our lives. Each book of the Bible has a structure that helps us in conjunction with its message to unfold the meaning of the book as God intended it. The study of the bible should be our life-long endeavor.

We should discuss our findings in the Bible with other people (Colossians 3:16). This will help us as well as them. The insight that we gain through our study of the Bible will help others to grow as we share it with them. It will also prepare the way for us to receive more light upon God's Word as we continue to study it. Perhaps some insight another person has will be the key to opening new doors for our understanding and growth also.

Finally, we must apply God's Word to our lives every day (Psalms 119:33). We must learn to live by it. It is not enough to have a bunch of facts about the Bible and about God. The point is that in knowing these facts they help us to walk with God and live in his ways and to do the work he has planned for us to do while we are here on earth. The Bible is the most important tangible thing we have to help us live life in a way that is acceptable to God.

It is a blessing from God to have a church in our communities. The local church building provides the people of God with a base from which to operate as we do the work God has instructed us to do throughout the world. The church, as we have already seen, tells us how to have a right relationship with God. It also tells us how to become more than we are now by use of the Bible which is the key to our spiritual growth.

The LIFE Network wants to help you make progress in your life and ministry for God. We want to help you experience the difference God can make in your life through the Bible that he has given to us. Would you be willing to make a commitment to read and study the Bible? Would you be willing to let us show you the way to do this? Let's tell God about this decision in prayer.

"Heavenly Father. Thank you for your Word. Thank you that you moved toward us by giving us this word so that we can know you, live for you, and help others to do the same. With your help, I commit to read and study your word. Help me to get into it. Help me to grow spiritually. Help me to become more than I am now. Help me to become all that you want me to be for your glory. In Jesus' name I pray. Amen."

MY SPIRITUAL GROWTH

I THE BIBLE IS OUR KEY FOR SPIRITUAL GROWTH
A. No ordinary book
  1. Comes from God
  2. Inspired by God
B. The writing of the Bible
  1. All about God
  2. How to know God
  3. How to live for God
C. The Bible is spiritually discerned
  1. God can conceal the truth
  2. God can reveal the truth

II HOW DOES SPIRITUAL GROWTH TAKE PLACE THROUGH USE OF THE BIBLE?
Four ways the Bible helps us grow spiritually
A. Doctrine
B. Reproof
C. Correction
D. Instruction

III WHAT SHOULD WE DO TO GROW SPIRITUALLY?
A. Read it
B. Believe it
C. Study it
D. Discuss it
E. Apply it

SCRIPTURES TO BROADEN YOUR UNDERSTANDING
1. Christians
   First called disciples (Acts 11:26)

2. Spiritual Food
   Hebrews 5:13-14

3. God's Word to us
   3 Peter 1:3-4

4. God's Word in us
   Colossians 3:16

LINES OF THEOLOGICAL CONNECTION
1. BIBLIOLOGY
   Inspiration of the Scriptures
   Illumination
   Revelation
   The Bible writers
   Canonization of the Scriptures
   Using Bible study tools

2. PNEUMATOLOGY
   Discernment

3. ANTHROPOLOGY
   Spiritual growth

LESSON GLOSSARY
1. Inspiration
   God-breathed

2. Reproof
   To address a fault

LESSON QUESTIONS

1. After we believe in Jesus Christ in our heart and receive his salvation, we must begin to grow spiritually. List some different ways we refer to this process of spiritual growth.

2. What is a disciple of Christ? A disciple of Christ is:

3. What one thing is our key to spiritual growth?

4. How did the Bible come to us?

20

5. How does the Holy Spirit help us to understand the Bible?

6. What kind of attitude should we have when we come to read and study the Bible?

7. What two words describe the Bible as food for our spiritual growth?

8. What kind of spiritual food from question 7 above do you need at this time in your life?

9. List 4 things the Bible is for us to help us grow spiritually.

10. List 5 things we need to do with our Bible to grow spiritually.

11. Do you have a copy of the Bible? If not, please let us know.

Allen L. Elder

3. MY PERSONAL MINISTRY FOR GOD

LESSON AIM: Show that God wants each one of us to have a personal ministry for him.

There are two statements that we often hear that each touch on the purpose of life but end up leaving us without a clue as to what to do or how to do it. Perhaps you have heard someone say something like this, "God has a wonderful purpose for your life." But, they cannot tell you very much about this purpose and how to find it, or how to fulfill it should you happen to find it. The other statement is just as bleak. They say, "I know God has left me here for a reason; I just don't know what it is."

Beyond this, there are also so many shallow interpretations that people offer for our purpose in life. Some say that the purpose for our life may be simply to open a door for a stranger or offer a smile to those who cross our paths every day. While these are admirable things to do, if they are ends in themselves, they are so far short of the purpose God had in mind when he created us and when he went to the extent of dying on the cross and rising from the dead.

The purpose of God for our lives can be seen in relation to the church (Ephesians 3:20-21). Let's take a look at three points which will help us to see how this is so.

It can be said that Christ has two bodies. The first one is the physical body that he had while he lived on the earth some 2,000 years ago. It is a body just like ours; one that grew physically, experienced fatigue, thirst, hunger, joy, sadness, pain, suffering, and even death (Philippians 2:5-8). Jesus still lives in that body today and in it, he is seated in heaven at the right hand of God, a place of power and authority.

Jesus also has a second body in which he lives today. This is his body, the church (Ephesians 1:19-23). In this body, Jesus lives just like we live in the world. We are an invisible personality living in a visible body. Everything we do in the world, we have to do through our body. God works in the world through his body, the church, in the same way. We are his feet, going to the places and to the peoples who have a need for him in their life. We are his hands, touching those who need a touch from God. We are his voice, bearing the news of his salvation to the lost of the world. He works through us as his body in the world.

God promised a blessing to all the peoples of the world (Genesis 12:1-3). This promise would be found in the person of the Lord Jesus Christ and the salvation that he made possible through his death on the cross and bodily resurrection from the dead. The news of this blessing would be carried to the nations of the world through his people. The Hebrew race had this privilege in the beginning. Through disobedience, they lost this privilege. At this time, the task has been given to his church. The church now has to accomplish this purpose of God on behalf of Christ and for the benefit of the nations (Matthew 28:18-20).

Taking the gospel to the nations obviously can be done in two ways. First, in the United States, the nations have come to us. People from other ethnic groups from all over the world now live in our neighborhoods. We go to the same schools. We shop in the same stores. We work at the same job sites. It is now possible to cross the ethnic boundaries of the nations without leaving our local towns, cities and counties. The nations have literally come to our doorsteps. In this way, God has made it easier for us to engage the nations with the gospel of the Lord Jesus Christ.

Another way to evangelize the nations is still by the old fashioned way; we can continue to go to where they are. To speak of the nations primarily is to speak of ethnic groups, not of geographical boundaries. But geographical boundaries are still part of the equation. When the nations are not within our physical reach, we can go to where they are. In recent years, many Christians have participated in short-term mission trips which have taken them into other countries where they have had the opportunity to take the gospel to the people in their homeland. This is a possibility that must be a part of our strategy of impacting the world with the gospel. We are to take the good news to the nations and make disciples of Christ. This is the practical purpose of the church in the world today.

The purpose of God for our life has to be thought of in two areas. The first area we can call God's general purpose for our life. The Bible tells us in no uncertain terms what God's general purpose is for our life. We do not have to guess at it or try to come up with a purpose on our own. God has called us out from the world that he might send us back into the world with the message of reconciliation through Jesus Christ (Mark 3:14) (John 17:18; 20:21). Those whom he calls out, after a period of spiritual development God sends out to the nations of the world with this good news of redemption and salvation. Upon hearing the gospel of Christ and believing in him, we are all to be engaged in the process of helping these new believers to become disciples, or learners and followers, of Jesus Christ. They too, in time, will do the same with others also (2Timothy 2:2). Christians refer to this purpose with the term, "The Great Commission". This is God's general purpose and it is the same for each and every follower of Christ (Matthew 28:18-20). There are no exclusions or exceptions.

The second area in which we are to think of God's purpose is in terms of his specific purpose for us as an individual. We are all intended to take the good news of salvation to all peoples of the world and to make disciples of the believers. The next thing we will have to determine is the specific way in which each of us will perform this task. God does not simply want us to do something for him; he wants us to do something specific for him (Ephesians 2:10). Therefore, we can say concerning the purpose of God that there is a track to follow, and there is a track to find.

We may think of God's purpose in terms of a railroad track. On one side, the track of God's general purpose has already been laid: he wants us to make disciples in all nations. It is up to us as individuals to lay the parallel track of our specific purpose in the unique way we will fulfill the Great Commission.

While the general purpose is clearly revealed to us in the Bible, the specific purpose for each of us is not. The specific purpose is the way that we as an individual will fulfill the great commission (1Corinthians 12:12-27). This is what we have to find along the way in life. The Bible does give us some clues to help us find this specific purpose. God has chosen the very place each one of us will occupy in the body of Christ. Another way to state this place is to refer to it as our personal ministry. To help us determine this place he has chosen, God has given us two things.

First, he has placed a desire within our heart that matches the works or ministry he wants us to accomplish in our place of service within the body of Christ (Psalms 37:3-5). It is easy to miss this clue since it is right under our nose. It is a legitimate consideration to think about

26

the things you really like and enjoy doing. This can be a clue to help us discover the way we can take the gospel to the nations in a way in which we would really enjoy doing it. It is possible to make a world-impacting ministry out of almost anything.

Another clue we have is our spiritual gift (Romans 12). When we were saved, God gave us a gift. This gift equips us to do the work that he has planned and for which he has given us a desire to accomplish. There are seven possible categories of spiritual gifts that we might have. And we have at least one of them. It is out of this gift and in conjunction with our heart's desire that we find the place God has designed for us in the body of Christ and consequently, the work, or the specific way in which we can fulfill his general purpose of making disciples in the nations of the world.

Yet another important part of the process of discovering our specific purpose is through an up-close, personal relationship with a more mature Christian (Philippians 1:1). We might call this person a mentor, a coach, or a teacher. A more Biblical title might be something like disciple-maker. Every Christian needs such a one in their life. We need this relationship to see a model of what we are to become and to help us grow. There is nothing that will be more beneficial to you in your maturing process and there is no substitute for it. It will make all the difference in the world in the progress you make along the way.

All of these clues (desire, spiritual gift, discipling relationship) have to be supported with your own personal study of the Bible and prayer. The Bible is the basis of all the ways God will speak to you. Prayer is how you will speak to him. Bible study and prayer are the means through which we commune, or fellowship with God (Ephesians 6:13-18). Through these, God will reveal his purpose for our life.

We are a part of Christ's church in the world. He wants us to take his good news to all peoples, making disciples of them for his sake. Each Christian has a key role to play in this effort. To fulfill our role, we must know God's general purpose and his specific purpose for our life.

These important discoveries do not fall upon us out of the sky. We will have to search for them. We will have to follow the clues we are given. We will have to journey to find them. It may be difficult. It may take a long time. But we can make the discovery. And, it will be worth it when we do. Let's ask God to help us find our way.

"*Heavenly Father. Thank you for making a special place in your church just for me. Thank you for showing us through the Bible, your general purpose of making disciples in all nations. Help me to find the specific way you would have me to fulfill this purpose. When I find it, help me to arrange my life around your purpose for as long as I may live. Help me to live my life for this greater cause and purpose. In Jesus' name I pray. Amen.*"

MY PERSONAL MINISTRY FOR GOD

I THE CHURCH IS THE BODY OF CHRIST IN THE WORLD TODAY
  A. Christ's physical body
  B. Christ's mystical body

II GOD'S PURPOSE FOR THE CHURCH IS TO TAKE HIS GOSPEL TO THE NATIONS
  A. The nations have come to us
  B. We can go to the nations

III AS A PART OF THE CHURCH, YOU HAVE A PURPOSE TO FULFILL
  A. God's general purpose for your life
  B. God's specific purpose for your life (clues to finding)
    1. The desire of our heart
    2. Our spiritual gift
    3. A discipling relationship
    4. Personal Bible study and prayer

SCRIPTURES TO BROADEN YOUR UNDERSTANDING
1. God's purpose for your life
   Matthew 28:18-20
   Acts 1:8
   1 Thessalonians 1:4

2. Jesus seated in heaven
   Colossians 3:1

3. God works through us
   2 Corinthians 5:20

4. God turns from the Jews to the church
   Romans 9-11

LINES OF THEOLOGICAL CONNECTION
1. ECCLESIOLOGY
   Preaching the gospel of Jesus Christ
   World Missions
   Disciple-making

2. CHRISTOLOGY
   Jesus lives in the believer

3. ANTHROPOLOGY
   The desire of the heart
   Spiritual gifts
   Personal relationship with God

LESSON GLOSSARY
1. Reconciliation
   To bring together

2. Mentor
   A personal guide

LESSON QUESTIONS

1. What is the best way to begin to understand God's purpose for your life?

2. List the two bodies of Christ in the world.

3. What is God's purpose for the church?

4. What are the two areas in which we can think of the

purpose of God?

5. What is another phrase for God's general purpose?

6. List two ways to take the gospel to the nations.

7. What are we referring to by the phrase, the specific purpose of God?

8. List four clues that will help you discover God's specific purpose for your life.

9. Have you discovered God's specific purpose for your life? If so, what is it?

10. What kind of ministry would you like to be involved in?

Allen L. Elder

4. MY IMPACT IN THE LIVES OF OTHERS

LESSON AIM: Show that God wants each one of us to share the good news of salvation through Jesus Christ with others.

SCRIPTURE: (1 John 1:4) Phillips

"We want you to be with us in this - in this fellowship with the Father, and Jesus Christ his Son. We must write and tell you about it, because the more that fellowship extends, the greater the joy it brings to us who are already in it."

It is a wonderful experience to grow in Christ. It is great to understand that the church can tell me how to have a right relationship with God, how to become more than I am now, and how to live for a greater purpose. The only thing as good as all of these is when we can help another person to make these discoveries also. This is another reason the church should be important to me; it helps me increase God's value in the world and the value of my life for God by helping others to learn these same things.

When we read the line above, we might protest. After all, God is infinite, isn't he? If he is infinite, is it possible that we can add to or take away from his value in the world, and if we can, how can we do it? The answer is, yes we can. It is possible for us to add to the value of

33

God in the world (John 17:4). And, since it is possible to add to his value, it is also possible to take away from his value in the world.

Consider how we can decrease the value of God in the world. Let's use two digits for a simple illustration; the numbers 0 and 1. Let the zero represent us since in ourselves and apart from Christ we are nothing. Let the 1 represent Jesus since he is whole and is to be first in all things. If I, as a zero place myself in front of the number 1, I decrease the value of the 1 by 100 times [.01]. If I influence another person to follow me in my own preeminence, we decrease the value of the 1 by 1,000 times [.001]. You can easily see how by influencing others in a negative way, we can bring discredit and decrease to the value of God through our life.

On the other hand, if we align our self properly in relation to Christ, we can increase his value in the world. A 0 on the right side of the 1 increases its value by 10 times [10]. Get another 0 and we increase its value by 100 times [100]. In the same way, we can increase the value of God in the world by proper alignment in relation to Jesus.

Just as you can increase the value of God in the world, you can increase the value of your own life by inviting others to follow you as you follow Christ. You do this first of all by giving them an example to follow (2Timothy 3:10-11). You model before them what it is to be a Christian. You open your life in such a way that you let them see how you interact with God. You let them see your struggles, your questions, your wrestling over the issues. You also let them see your faith in God and his Word. You show them how you pray and believe God for the things you commit to him. You let them see your confidence and hope in the Lord. You show them how to read and study the Bible and how to pray. You let them watch you and work with you as you work in the lives of others in all kinds of situations. In doing so, by the influence of your own life you press into them the image of Christ himself. Before long, they begin to understand that they can live in the same way. After a while, you will have found another zero that you can line up with yourself beside Christ, increasing both his value and yours in the world.

While you model the Christian life before them, you also teach them all that you know about Christ and his way of life (Colossians 1:28-29). You get them involved in the Scriptures, reading them and studying them. You show them how to connect the dots between the stories of the people in the Bible with Christ himself. You teach them to rely upon the Holy Spirit as they study the Word. You show them how to use tools for Bible study. You call upon them to look deeper and to see more from the text. You help them to see the relevance and to make personal application of the ancient Scriptures in their life today. You feed them the milk of the Word until it becomes the meat of the Word.

Next, you give them little pieces of the work to do themselves (Luke 10). They can try out the things they have learned while you are there to guide them along. If they make a mistake, you are there to correct them. If they miss the point of it all, you can call their attention to this and steer them in the right way. If they make a total flop, you can pick them up, dust them off, and give them another opportunity to try it again. Pretty soon, they will have it and will be able to do the work without your direct supervision.

Finally, when you have brought them far enough along, you turn them loose to do the same thing with others, requiring them to do the same thing with others. Through this multiplying effort, spiritual reproduction takes place. Continual reproduction is insured into the future. Paul told Timothy, "What you have heard of me in the presence of many witnesses, the same commit thou to faithful men who shall be able to teach others also"

(Timothy 2:2). Through the multiplication of other disciples of Christ, you increase the value of God in the world, you increase your own value in the world, you fulfill the Lord's Great Commission, you help other people to have true joy in their life, and you bring joy to yourself and to other Christians. These are among the endless benefits of investing your life into other people with a goal of spiritual reproduction. This is how you can increase the value of your own life for God.

You are a fortunate individual if you have a church in your community that is working to help you know and understand why the church should be important to you in helping you get your life on track. The church is important because it tells you how to have a right relationship with God, it tells you how to become much more than you are now, it tells you how to live your life for a greater purpose, and it tells you how to increase the value of your life for God by helping others to make these same discoveries. Your life can count in a significant way for the glory of God. You can make your mark in the world by being a part of a great commission-minded church in your community. In the body of Christ, we can become more and accomplish more in the world for God's glory. We encourage you to find a church in your community where you can join in the work God is doing in the world. Pray this prayer from your heart to God.

"*Our Father. Thank you that I can increase the value of your life and mine in the world through reproducing more followers of Christ. Help me to learn this process and to live it in all of my relationships with other people. Please lead me to a church where I can learn, grow, and serve. In Jesus' name I pray. Amen.*"

MY IMPACT IN THE LIVES OF OTHERS

I YOU CAN INCREASE GOD'S VALUE IN THE WORLD
    A. Decreasing God's value - Putting ourself before God
    B. Increasing God's value - Putting God first

II YOU CAN INCREASE YOUR VALUE IN THE WORLD
    A. Be a model others can follow
    B. Teach others to follow Christ
    C. Assign work and check behind them
    D. Require them to reproduce other Christ followers

SCRIPTURES TO BROADEN YOUR UNDERSTANDING
1. Bringing God glory
   John 17:4

2. Multiplying your life
   2 Timothy 2:2

LINES OF THEOLOGICAL CONNECTION
1. DISCIPLE-MAKING
   Modeling
   Multiplication

2. EVANGELISM
   Soul-winning
   Sharing the gospel

Allen L. Elder

LESSON QUESTIONS

1. We all at times have done things to decrease God's value in the world. Are you seeking now to increase God's value in the world, and if so, how?

2. Can you name a person who has had a spiritual influence in your life?

3. Who do you know that would be willing to have you make a spiritual investment into their life?

4. What will you do to make an effort to make that investment into their life?

5. A FINAL WORD

The four lessons you have just read is a simple summary of the Christian life. To use another analogy, these are the four corner pieces of the puzzle of your life which you need to have in place in order to get your life on track for the glory of God and for fulfilling God's purpose for your life here on earth. You will never have a better explanation or opportunity to begin to move your life into the right direction than you have right now by getting these things in place in your life. Get them in place and begin to get your life on track today. Again, the four corners are:

1. Make sure you have a personal relationship with God through his Son, Jesus Christ.

2. Grow in the grace and knowledge of the Lord Jesus Christ.

3. Discover, develop, and deploy yourself in your own personal ministry for God.

4. Be a witness for Christ, sharing the gospel, winning the lost, and making disciples of Christ among the nations.

Allen L. Elder

Once these corners are in place, you have the rest of your life to fill in all the other pieces of the puzzle. These corner pieces are a guide to finding all the other pieces and getting them into the right places as well. There will be times in your life when you feel like your life has gotten off track. Do not panic. Simply go back to these four corners, or pillars and find where the problem lies, fix it, and get on track again. This sounds so simple and easy and looks good on paper, I know. This is not to say that finding all the other pieces of the puzzle of your life, keeping your life on track, or getting it back on track when it derails will be easy. Sometimes it will be hard, even extremely difficult. And it will require lots of work. This is just the way it is. But it is not impossible as you may have previously thought, and you can do it. So, do it.

I am very interested in hearing how this book helped you get your life on track and keep it there. My email address is at the end of this book. Please share your story with me. I look forward to hearing from you very soon.

Allen L. Elder

ANSWERS KEY TO LESSON QUESTIONS

CHAPTER 1
QUESTIONS ANSWER KEY

1. What are some beautiful sights you have seen in the created world?
Students answer.

2. Name some things that you enjoy about people.
Students answer.

3. Do you know your own ethnic background?
Students answer.

4. List some of the ethnic groups in your community.
Students answer.

5. Sin is devastating, not simply because of the things we do, but because of the condition into which we are born. List three results of our sinful condition.
In sin, we are spiritually dead, separated from God, and unable to come to God on our own.

6. What is the only solution God will accept for our sin problem?
Jesus Christ and his death is the only sacrifice for man's sin that God accepts.

7. How does God's solution for our sin problem come to us?
We are saved by grace, through faith in Christ.

8. Jesus died on the cross for our sins and he arose from the dead. The Bible calls this the gospel, or good news. List two ways that God moves us to respond to the gospel.
We have to believe on Jesus in our heart, and we have to confess Jesus with our mouth.

GETTING MY LIFE ON TRACK

9. Have you believed on Jesus for salvation?
Students answer.

10. Would you like to speak with someone about your decision to trust Christ?
Students answer.

CHAPTER 2
QUESTIONS ANSWER KEY
1. After we believe in Jesus Christ in our heart and receive his salvation, we must begin to grow spiritually. List some different ways we refer to this process of spiritual growth.
   a. Growing in Christ
   b. Spiritual growth
   c. Spiritual development
   d. Maturing in Christ
   e. Discipleship

2. What is a disciple of Christ? A disciple of Christ is:
   a. A learner
   b. A follower

3. What one thing is our key to spiritual growth?
The Bible

4. How did the Bible come to us?
   a. From God
   b. Through Man

5. How does the Holy Spirit help us to understand the Bible?
By illumination - giving us spiritual light in order to see and understand.

6. What kind of attitude should we have when we come to read and study the Bible?
With humility and dependence upon God

7. What two words describe the Bible as food for our spiritual growth?
a. Milk
b. Meat

8. What kind of spiritual food from question 7 above do you need at this time in your life? Student response

9. List 4 things the Bible is for us to help us grow spiritually.
a. Doctrine
b. Reproof
c. Correction
d. Instruction

10. List 5 things we need to do with our Bible to grow spiritually.
a. Read it
b. Believe it
c. Study it
d. Discuss it
e. Apply it

11. Do you have a copy of the Bible? If not, please let us know.
Student response

CHAPTER 3
QUESTIONS ANSWER KEY

1. What is the best way to begin to understand God's purpose for your life?
In relation to the church

2. List the two bodies of Christ in the world.
a. His physical body.
b. His spiritual body - the church.

3. What is God's purpose for the church?
To take the gospel to the nations.

4. What are the two areas in which we can think of the purpose of God?
a. His general purpose.
b. His specific purpose.

5. What is another phrase for God's general purpose?
The Great Commission

6. List two ways to take the gospel to the nations.
a. The nations come to us
b. We can go to the nations

7. What are we referring to by the phrase, the specific purpose of God?
The way an individual will fulfill the great commission

8. List four clues that will help you discover God's specific purpose for your life.
a. Desire
b. Spiritual gift
c. Relationship with a disciple-maker
d. Personal Bible study

9. Have you discovered God's specific purpose for your life? If so, what is it?
Student response

10. What kind of ministry would you like to be involved in?
Student response

CHAPTER 4
QUESTIONS ANSWER KEY
1. We all at times have done things to decrease God's value in the world. Are you seeking now to increase God's value in the world, and if so, how?
Student response

2. Can you name a person who has had a spiritual influence in your life?
Student response

3. Who do you know that would be willing to have you make a spiritual investment
into their life?
Student response

4. What will you do to make an effort to make that investment into their life?
Student response

ABOUT THE AUTHOR

Rev. Allen L. Elder is an ordained pastor serving Southern Baptist churches in his home state of South Carolina for over thirty years. His ministry focus is upon personal disciple-making in fulfilment of the Lord's great commission. Allen is a husband, father, grand-father, and a United States Air Force Veteran. He welcomes your response to his writings. Allen can be contacted by email at allenelder@att.net.

Made in the USA
Middletown, DE
22 August 2024